MOSES AND THE TEN PLAGUES

Activity Book for Beginners

Moses and the Ten Plagues Activity Book for Beginners

Bible Pathway Adventures® is a trademark of BPA Publishing Ltd.
Defenders of the Faith® is a trademark of BPA Publishing Ltd.

ISBN: 978-1-98-858587-1

Author: Pip Reid

Creative Director: Curtis Reid

For free Bible resources including coloring pages, worksheets, puzzles and more, visit our website at:

shop.biblepathwayadventures.com

Introduction for Parents

Enjoy teaching your children about the Bible with our *Moses and the Ten Plagues Activity Book for Beginners*. Packed with lesson plans, worksheets, coloring pages, and puzzles to help educators just like you teach children a Biblical faith. Includes scripture references for easy Bible verse look-up and a handy answer key for teachers.

Bible Pathway Adventures helps educators teach children a Biblical faith in a fun and creative way. We do this via our Activity Books and free printable activities – available on our website: www.biblepathwayadventures.com

Thanks for buying this Activity Book and supporting our ministry. Every book purchased helps us continue our work providing free Classroom Packs and discipleship resources to families and missions everywhere.

The search for Truth is more fun than Tradition!

Table of Contents

LESSON 1 | Lesson Plan
Moses and the princess

Teacher: _____

Today's Bible passage: Exodus 2:1-10

Welcome prayer:
Pray a simple prayer with the children before you begin the lesson.

Lesson objectives:
In this lesson, children will learn:
1. Why Pharaoh wanted to kill the Hebrew baby boys
2. How Moses' mother saved her own baby boy

Did You Know?
The name Moses means 'to draw out' because he was drawn out of the water (Exodus 2:10).

Bible lesson overview:
A long time ago in the land of Egypt, a Hebrew baby named Moses was born. But there was just one problem. The king of Egypt (the Pharaoh) did not like the Hebrews. "Kill all the Hebrew baby boys!" he said. "But let the baby girls live." To hide Moses from the Pharaoh, his mother put him in a basket by the riverbank. Moses' sister watched to make sure he was safe. Later that day, the king's daughter (the princess) found Moses. She asked Moses' mother to take care of him. When Moses was older, he went to live at the palace with the princess.

Let's Review:

Questions to ask your students:

1. Who was the king of Egypt?
2. Where was Moses born?
3. How did Moses' mother hide him from Pharaoh?
4. Who watched to see if Moses was safe?
5. Who did the princess ask to take care of baby Moses?

 A memory verse to help children remember God's Word:

By faith, Moses parents hid him.." (Hebrews 11:23)

 Activities:

Worksheet: The number three
Worksheet: King of Egypt
Worksheet: Land of Egypt
Worksheet: My family
Finish the drawing: Baby Moses
Worksheet: Match the picture
Map activity: Where is Egypt?
Labyrinth: Baby Moses
Worksheet: E is for Egypt
Bible puzzle: Who was Moses?
Worksheet: W is for water

 Closing prayer:
End the lesson with a small prayer.

3 three

Moses' mother hid him
for three months.

3 3 3 3 3 3 3

Write the number three in the boxes below.

How many fingers are there?

Who hid Moses for three months?

....

King of Egypt

The Pharaoh was the king of Egypt. Trace the word 'king'.
Color the objects that start with the letter 'k'.

lion

kid

key

kettle

🌿 Land of Egypt 🌿

Moses lived in the land of Egypt. Trace the triangles.
Trace the pyramids.

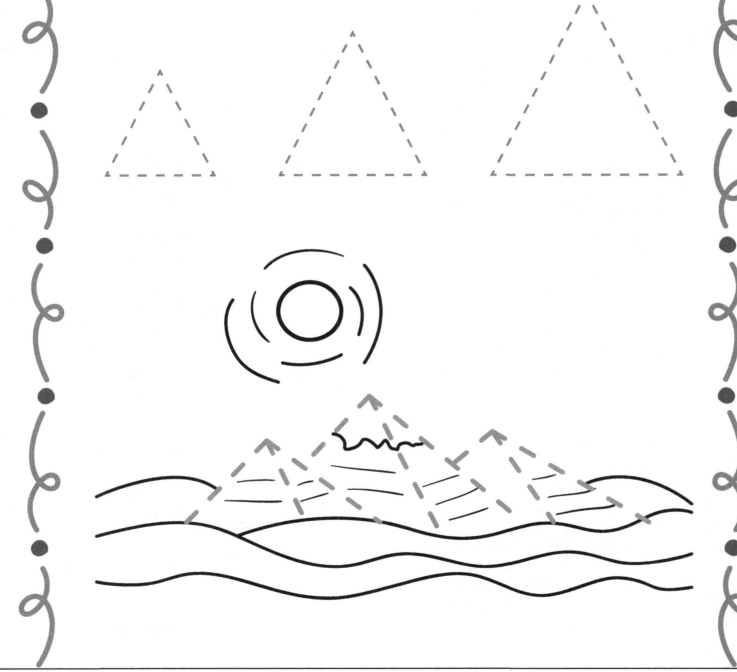

My family

Moses had a mom and a dad, a sister (Miriam) and a brother (Aaron). What does your family look like? Draw your family below.

☙ Finish the Drawing ☙

Moses' mother put Moses in a basket to hide
him from Pharaoh. Draw baby Moses in the basket.

🌿 Where is Egypt? 🌿

Moses grew up in the land of Egypt.
Color the land of Egypt green.

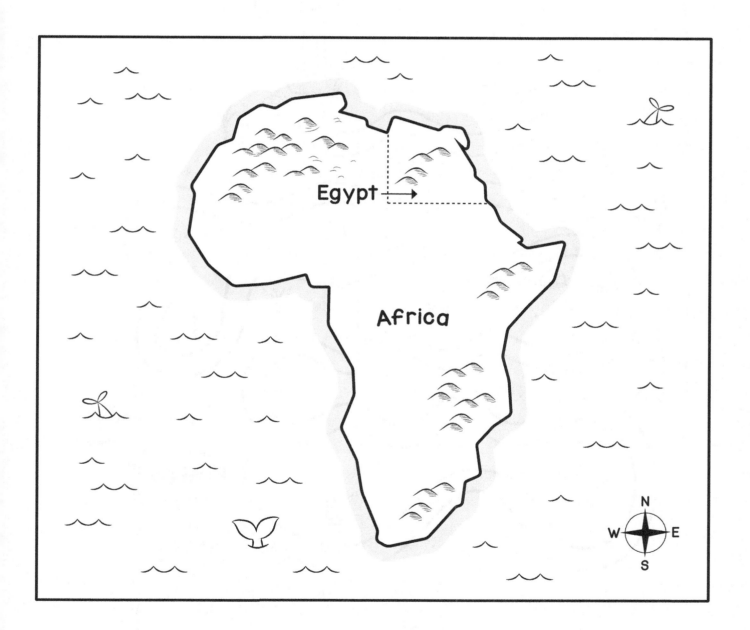

🌿 Baby Moses 🌿

Help Moses find his way to the princess.

Start

Finish

✦ E is for Egypt ✦

Moses was born in the land of Egypt.
Trace the letter and sentence. Color the picture.

egypt

E is for Egypt

❧ Who was Moses? ❧

Fill in the blanks using the chart below. What do you see?

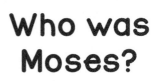

13 15 19 5 19

23 1 19   1

8 5 2 18 5 23

A	B	C	D	E	F	G	H	I	J	K	L	M
1	2	3	4	5	6	7	8	9	10	11	12	13

N	O	P	Q	R	S	T	U	V	W	X	Y	Z
14	15	16	17	18	19	20	21	22	23	24	25	26

✷ W is for water ✷

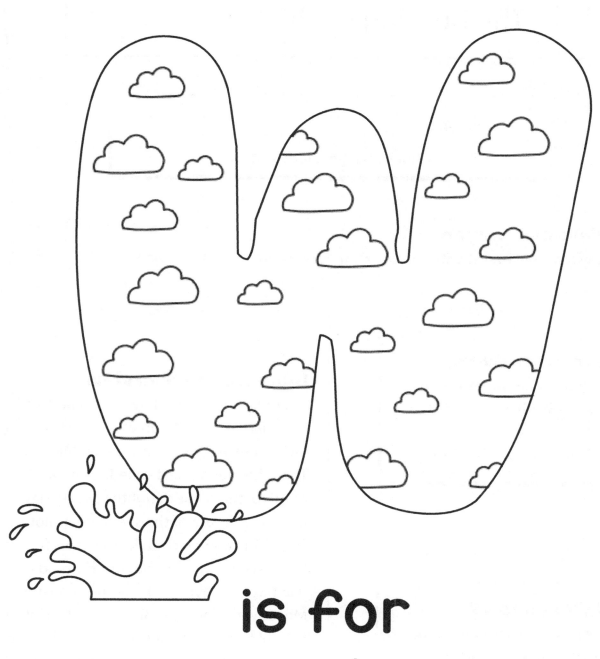

is for

water

LESSON 2 | Lesson Plan
The burning bush

Teacher: _____

Today's Bible passage: Exodus 3:1-10

Welcome prayer:
Pray a simple prayer with the children before you begin the lesson.

Lesson objectives:
In this lesson, children will learn:
1. Moses' job while he lived in the land of Midian
2. God's instructions to Moses

Did You Know?
Moses was a shepherd in the land of Midian for forty years.

Bible lesson overview:
While Moses lived in Egypt, he killed an Egyptian man. Pharaoh was not happy! So, Moses ran away to a land called Midian. There he met a priest called Jethro and married one of his daughters. Every day Moses took care of the sheep near Mount Sinai. One day, God spoke to Moses from a bush that was on fire but not burning up. "Go back to Egypt and free the Israelites!" But Moses was scared. "I cannot speak nicely. The king of Egypt will not listen to me," he said. "Do not worry," said God. "I AM who I AM. I will be with you. The king will let you go."

Let's Review:

Questions to ask your students:

1. What did Moses do every day in Midian?
2. Where did Moses take care of Jethro's sheep?
3. What was strange about the bush that Moses saw?
4. Why was Moses nervous to speak to Pharaoh?
5. What did God tell Moses to do? (Exodus 3:10)

 A memory verse to help children remember God's Word:

"God said to Moses, "I AM WHO I AM" (Exodus 3:14)

 Activities:

Wanted worksheet: Moses
Map activity: Escape to Midian
Bible activity: Mount Sinai
Worksheet: What a lot of animals!
Craft activity: The burning bush
Coloring page: "I will be with you."
Worksheet: Trace the Words
Bible word search puzzle: The burning bush
Worksheet: My feet
Let's learn Hebrew: Moses
Bible craft: Let's make a sheep!

 Closing prayer:
End the lesson with a small prayer.

WANTED

Name:...............................

🌿 Escape to Midian 🌿

Moses killed an Egyptian man. Pharaoh was not happy!
So, Moses ran away to the land of Midian.
Connect the dots to show Moses the way to Midian.

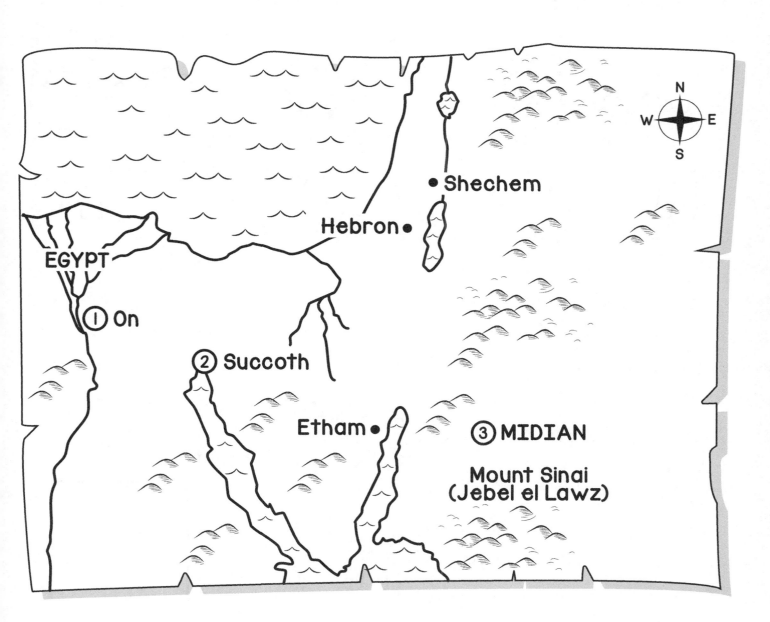

🌿 What a lot of animals! 🌿

A shepherd takes care of his animals.
What animals did Moses care for?
Count the animals and write the number in the box.

🌿 The burning bush 🌿

Glue pieces of red, yellow, and orange tissue paper
onto the bush to make a burning bush!

"I will be with YOU.,,

(Exodus 3:12)

Trace the Words

Color the pictures.

bush

fire

sheep

snake

🌿 The burning bush 🌿

Find and circle each of the words from the list below.

S	I	Q	G	B	G
G	N	G	O	U	O
P	Z	A	D	S	A
I	K	U	K	H	T
F	I	R	E	E	W
S	H	E	E	P	C

FIRE GOD
SHEEP BUSH
SNAKE GOAT

❧ My feet ❧

In the desert, Moses wore sandals on his feet.
Why do you think God told Moses to take them off?
Circle and color the things you wear on your feet.

✶ Mosheh ✶

The Hebrew name for Moses is Mosheh.
Moses lived in the land of Midian for 40 years.

Mosheh

מֹשֶׁה

Moses

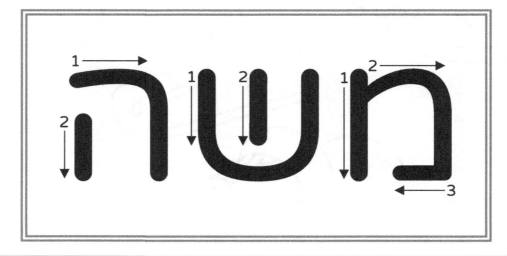

Let's write!

Practice writing Moses' Hebrew name on the lines below.

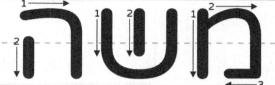

Try this on your own.
Remember that Hebrew is read from RIGHT to LEFT.

LESSON 3

Lesson Plan
The plagues

Teacher: _____

Today's Bible passage: Exodus 7:14-10:29

(parents: when you teach this section, shorten the Bible passage by focusing on one plague)

Welcome prayer:
Pray a simple prayer with the children before you begin the lesson.

Lesson objectives:
In this lesson, children will learn:
1. How God kept the Israelites safe from the plagues
2. The names of the first nine plagues

Did You Know?
The plagues showed Pharaoh and the Egyptians how useless their gods were compared to God.

Bible lesson overview:
Moses and Aaron went to see the king of Egypt. They said, "The God of Israel says, 'Let My people go so that they may hold a feast to Me in the wilderness.'" The king laughed and said, "No!" So, God sent ten plagues on the land of Egypt. Each plague was worse than the last one. First, God turned the Nile River to blood. Then He sent a plague of frogs. The king still did not free the Israelites, so God sent plagues of lice, flies, boils, sickness, and hailstones on fire. But He did not send the plagues on the Israelites who lived in the land of Goshen. Next, God sent a plague of locusts. And He made it very dark in Egypt for three days. But the king still said, "No!"

Let's Review:

Questions to ask your students:

1. Who asked Pharaoh to free the Israelites?
2. What was the first plague?
3. Where did God keep the Israelites safe?
4. How many days was the land of Egypt in darkness?
5. How many plagues were there?

 A memory verse to help children remember God's Word:

"Let My people go!" (Exodus 7:16)

Activities:

Tracing map: Where is Pharaoh's palace?
Bible activity: Moses and Aaron meet Pharaoh
Worksheet: The number ten
Connect the dots: Plague of frogs
Bible activity: First five plagues
Bible activity: Second five plagues
Trace the Words: The ten plagues
Worksheet: What a lot of plagues!
Worksheet: What's my sound?
Worksheet: True or false?
Worksheet: M is for Moses

 Closing prayer:
End the lesson with a small prayer.

Where is Pharaoh's palace?

Help Moses and Aaron find Pharaoh's palace.

The Number 10

God sent ten plagues on Egypt.
Trace the numbers. Circle and color the objects.

10 10 10 10 10 10 10

Circle 10 flies

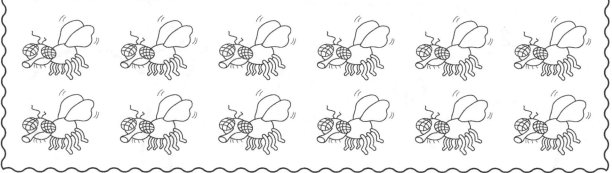

Color 10 lice

Plague of frogs

Connect the dots to see the picture.

🌿 Trace the Words 🌿

Color the pictures.

Trace the Words

Color the pictures.

Trace the Words

Color the pictures.

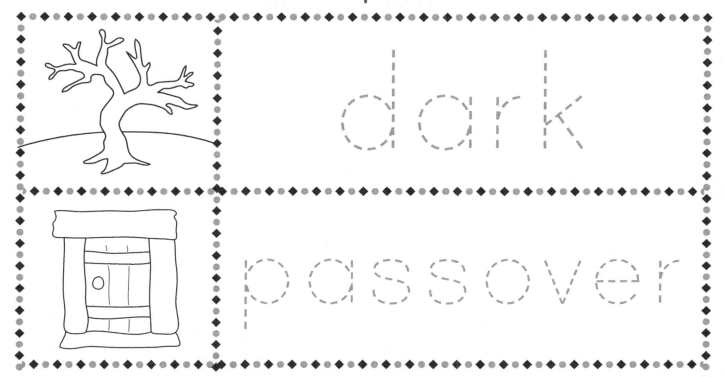

🌿 The ten plagues 🌿

What a lot of plagues!
Can you count them and write the number?

blood

locust

hail

lice

cow

boils

frog

death of firstborn

fly

darkness

🌿 What's my sound? 🌿

The word 'plague' starts with the letter P.
Circle and color the pictures that have
the same beginning sound as Plague.

pumpkin

plum

plane

pizza

tree

☙ True or false? ❧

Listen to the statements. Are they true or false?

God sent a plague of dogs	God sent 15 plagues
God turned the Nile river to blood	God made it dark for five days
God sent a plague of frogs	Moses and Zipporah met Pharaoh

M is for Moses

Moses and Aaron asked Pharaoh to free the Israelites (Exodus 7:10). Trace the letters. Color the picture.

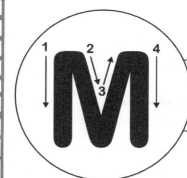

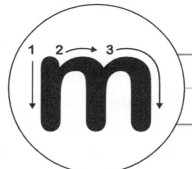

 Trace the letter m

 Color Moses

Moses

LESSON 4 | Lesson Plan
The Passover

Teacher: _____

Today's Bible passage: Exodus 12:1-28

Welcome prayer:
Pray a simple prayer with the children before you begin the lesson.

Lesson objectives:
In this lesson, children will learn:
1. What the Israelites ate for the first Passover meal
2. How the Israelites were saved from the final plague

Did You Know?
Yeshua was crucified on Passover, 1500 years after the first Passover in Egypt.

Bible lesson overview:
God sent one last plague - the death of first-born males and animals in Egypt. Before He did this, He told the Israelites to eat a meal of bitter herbs and lamb (the lamb must only be one year old), and to put the lamb's blood on the doorposts of their houses. If they did this, their families would be safe and no one would die. God also told them to eat bread without yeast (matzah) for seven days. That night, God visited Egypt. Everywhere He saw blood on the doorposts, He passed over that house. But the Pharaoh's son died. After this happened, the Pharaoh wanted the Israelites gone! He told them to take their belongings and leave Egypt.

Let's Review:

Questions to ask your students:

1. What was the last plague?
2. What did the Israelites eat for the Passover meal?
3. How old was the lamb that the Israelites ate for the Passover meal?
4. What type of bread did God tell the Israelites to eat for seven days?
5. How did God keep the Israelites safe from the last (tenth) plague?

 A memory verse to help children remember God's Word:

"…when I see the blood, I will pass over you." (Exodus 12:13)

 ## Activities:

Coloring page: The Passover
Worksheet: Counting practice
Worksheet: What do you eat for the Passover?
Passover flashcards
Coloring activity: The Passover
Worksheet: What's the Word?
Worksheet: M is for matzah
Worksheet: What's different?
Worksheet: I Spy!
Bible word search puzzle: The Passover
Worksheet: The number seven
Bible craft: Ten plagues necklace

 ## Closing prayer:

End the lesson with a small prayer.

The Passover

🌿 Counting practice 🌿

Color the square with the correct number
of objects in each box.

blood
| 2 |
| 5 |
| 3 |

lamb
| 1 |
| 5 |
| 4 |

bush
| 2 |
| 3 |
| 4 |

bread
| 3 |
| 6 |
| 1 |

What do you eat for the Passover?

Draw the food you eat.

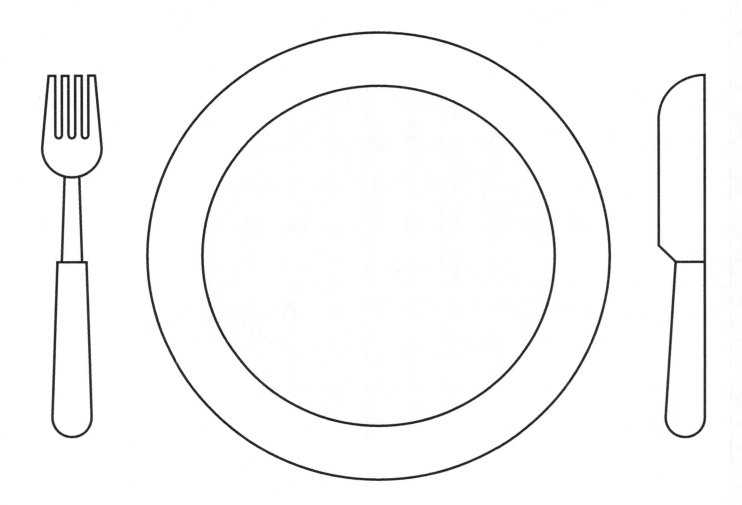

The Passover

God told the Israelites to put blood on the doorposts of their houses. Draw blood on the top and sides of the door.

🌿 What's the Word? 🌿

Draw a line to the picture it matches with.

1. matzah

2. blood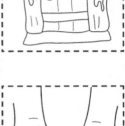

3. lamb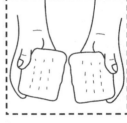

4. Moses

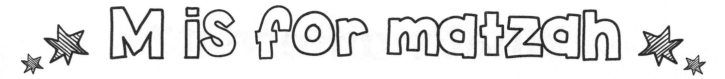

M is for matzah

The Hebrew word for unleavened bread is matzah. Matzah is a type of bread made from flour and water. Trace the words. Color the picture.

M is for matzah

🌿 What's different? 🌿

Circle the picture that is different.

❧ I spy! ❧

Color the same objects a single color. Then count each type of object and write the number on the label.

❧ The Passover ❧

Find and circle each of the words from the list below.

```
C U P H D L
M R L E O A
S C F R O M
Z K P B R B
B R E A D B
F E E T B D
```

HERB   FEET
CUP   LAMB
DOOR   BREAD

7 seven

God told the Israelites to eat bread
without yeast for seven days (Exodus 13:6).

Write the number seven in the boxes below.

How many fingers are there?

Do you like to eat bread without yeast (matzah)?

....

LESSON 5 | Lesson Plan
Red Sea crossing

Teacher: _____

Today's Bible passages: Exodus 13:17-22 and 14:19-29

Welcome prayer:
Pray a simple prayer with the children before you begin the lesson.

Lesson objectives:
In this lesson, children will learn:
1. How God led the Israelites through the desert
2. How God saved the Israelites from the Egyptians

Did You Know?
Explorers have found old Egyptian chariot wheels and animal skeletons at the bottom of the Red Sea.

Bible lesson overview:
The Israelites followed Moses out of Egypt. God used a tall cloud during the day and a pillar of fire at night to show them the way to go. Soon they reached the Red Sea. Meanwhile, the king of Egypt was angry the Israelites were gone. He sent his army to chase after them. When the Israelites saw the army, they were scared. But God opened up the water so they could walk along dry ground to the other side of the Red Sea. When the Egyptians did the same thing, the water crashed down on them and they all drowned. The Israelites were safe!

Let's Review:

Questions to ask your students:

1. How did God show the Israelites the way across the desert?
2. Why were the Israelites afraid?
3. How did God part the Red Sea?
4. How did the Israelites get to the other side of the Red Sea?
5. What happened to the Egyptians when they tried to cross the Red Sea?

 A memory verse to help children remember God's Word:

"…the Israelites went through the sea on dry ground." (Exodus 14:29)

Activities:

Coloring page: Let My people go…
Coloring page: Leaving Egypt
Worksheet: The king of Egypt
Worksheet: Pharaoh's chariots
Bible craft: Pharaoh's horses
Worksheet: Let's draw!
Tracing map: Cross the Red Sea
Worksheet: Let's go!
Connect the dots: Moses
Bible activity: Help the Israelites cross the Red Sea
Worksheet: Wet & dry
Certificate of Award

 Closing prayer:

End the lesson with a small prayer.

⚘ Leaving Egypt ⚘

The Israelites left Egypt with their unbaked bread.
Draw a sun in the sky. Color the picture.

🌿 The king of Egypt 🌿

Pharaoh was the king of Egypt. He let the Israelites go!
Trace the words. Color the picture.

The king of Egypt

Pharaoh's chariots

Pharaoh and his army chased after the Israelites in chariots (Exodus 14:9). Trace the circles.

🌿 Let's Draw! 🌿

Pharaoh chased after the Israelites with his horses and chariots (Exodus 14:9). Draw a scene from this Bible passage.

Cross the Red Sea

Help the Israelites cross the
Red Sea by tracing the lines.

✶ Let's go! ✶

Read Exodus 12:35-39 with your children. What did the Israelites take with them when they left Egypt? Circle and color the correct pictures below.

🌿 Moses 🌿

Moses led the Israelites out of Egypt.
Connect the dots to see the picture.

Help the Israelites
cross the Red Sea

Ask children questions about the lesson.
When they answer correctly, they can color a square and
move through the Red Sea until they reach the other side.

Wet & dry

The Israelites crossed the sea on dry land (Exodus 14:29). Water is wet. Land is dry.

Draw something wet.

Draw something dry.

CRAFTS & PROJECTS

✿ Match the picture ✿

Color and cut out the pictures.
Place each picture above the correct word.

baby

princess

king

basket

❧ Mount Sinai ☙

Moses took care of Jethro's sheep and goats near
Mount Sinai. Color and cut out Moses and the animals.
Paste them around the mountain.

Moses

goat

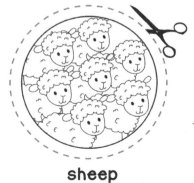

sheep

🍃 Let's make a sheep! 🍃

You will need:
1. Paper plates
2. White cotton balls
3. Black construction paper
4. Craft animal eyes
5. School glue

Preparation: Cut out the sheep face, legs, and ears from the template on the next page.

Instructions:

1. Cover a paper plate with school glue.
2. Cover the school glue with white cotton balls.
3. Help your child assemble the sheep's face using the sheep template pieces and craft eyes.
4. Glue the sheep's head and legs to the cotton ball body.

1.   *2.*   *3.*

ta-da!

Moses and Aaron meet Pharaoh

Color and cut out the people. Glue them inside Pharaoh's palace.

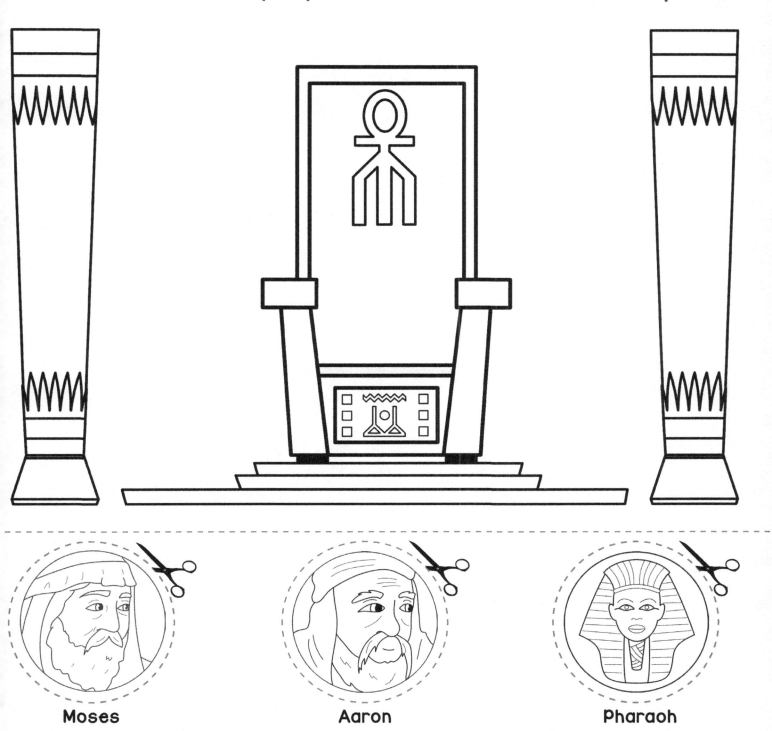

Moses

Aaron

Pharaoh

The first five plagues

God sent ten plagues on Egypt. The first five plagues were blood, frogs, lice, flies, and dead cows. Cut out a word at the bottom of the page. Place it next to the correct picture.

blood ✂

frog ✂

lice ✂

fly ✂

dead cow ✂

🌿 Five more plagues... 🌿

God sent ten plagues on Egypt. The last five plagues were boils, hail, locusts, darkness, and death of firstborn. Cut out a word at the bottom of the page. Place it next to the correct picture.

boils ✂ hail ✂ locust ✂

death of
first born ✂ darkness ✂

🌿 Passover flashcards 🌿

Color and cut out the flashcards.
Hang them around your home or classroom.

egypt

5

goat

6

blood

7

matzah

8

www.biblepathwayadventures.com
Moses and the Ten Plagues (Beginners)

Ten Plagues necklace

You will need:
1. Ten plagues pictures (see next pages)
2. Paint, felt pens, or crayons
3. Hole punch
4. Yarn or string

Instructions:

1. Have your children color the pictures of the ten plagues.
2. Cut out the pictures (children may need to help with this step).
3. Use a hole punch to create a hole in each of the circles.
4. String the circles with yarn or string to create a ten plagues necklace.

ta-da!

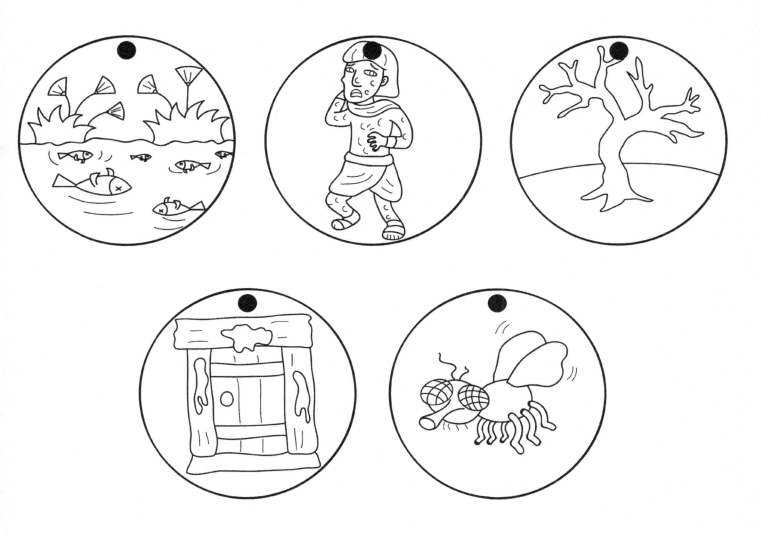

Pharaoh's horses

Pharaoh wanted the Israelites back! He sent all his horses and chariots, horsemen and soldiers to get them. Let's make a horse.

You will need:
1. Clothespins
2. Black string
3. Paint or felt pens
4. Heavy card stock
5. Glue sticks or paste

Instructions:

1. Print or copy the horse template onto heavy card stock. Color the horse pieces.
2. Cut out the horse pieces and glue both sides together. Color two clothespins brown. Paint the bottom of the clothespins black for hooves.
3. Glue black string onto the horse to create a tail. Add the clothespins to the horse body.

ta-da!

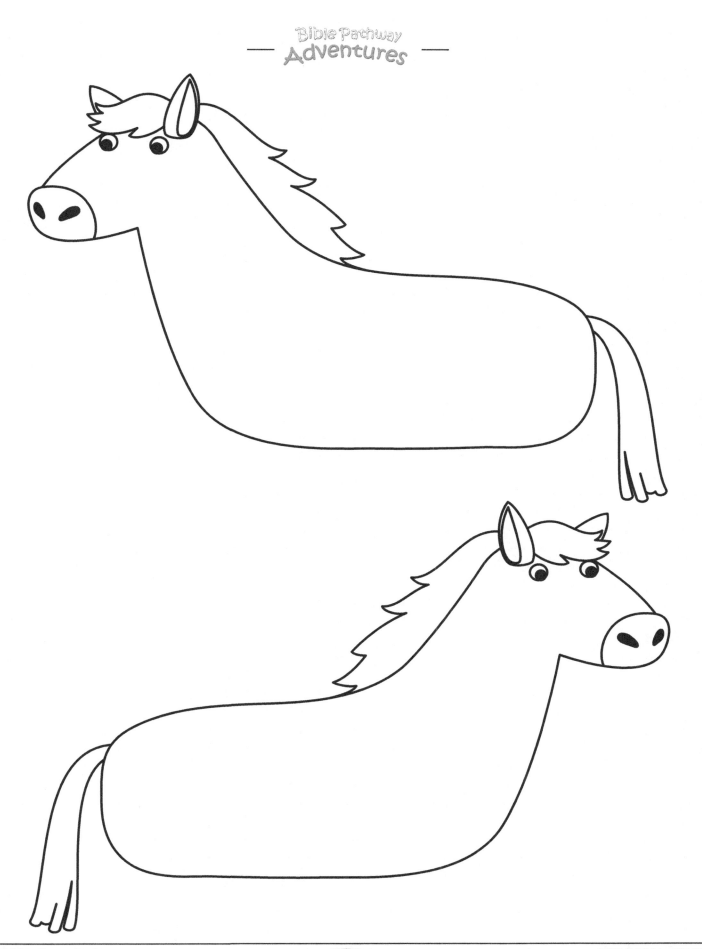

www.biblepathwayadventures.com
Moses and the Ten Plagues (Beginners)

❧ Certificate of Award ❧

Certificate of Award

Congratulations

For

Signed

ANSWER KEY

LESSON ONE: Moses and the princess
Let's Review answers:
1. Pharaoh
2. The land of Egypt
3. Moses' mother put him in a basket by the Nile river
4. Miriam (Moses' sister)
5. A Hebrew woman (Moses' mother)

LESSON TWO: The Burning Bush
Let's Review answers:
1. He took care of the sheep
2. Mount Sinai
3. It was on fire but not burning up
4. Because Moses could not speak well
5. Go back to Egypt and free the Israelites

LESSON THREE: The Plagues
Let's Review answers:
1. Moses and Aaron
2. Plague of blood
3. Land of Goshen
4. Three days
5. Ten plagues

Worksheet: True or false?
God sent a plague of dogs (false)
God sent 15 plagues (false)
God turned the Nile river to blood (true)
God made it dark for five days (false)
God sent a plague of frogs (true)
Moses and Zipporah met Pharaoh (false)

LESSON FOUR: The Passover
Let's Review answers:
1. Death of first-born males and animals
2. Lamb and bitter herbs
3. One-year old male lamb
4. Unleavened bread (matzah)
5. They put blood on their doorposts

LESSON FIVE: Red Sea crossing
Let's Review answers:
1. Pillar of fire by night and a pillar of cloud by day
2. The Israelites thought they were trapped and the Egyptians would catch them
3. He told Moses to stretch out his hand over the sea
4. They ran along dry ground between two walls of water
5. The Egyptians drowned in the Red Sea

Discover more Activity Books!

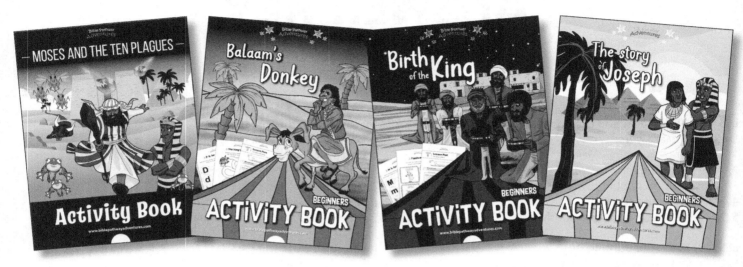

Available for purchase at shop.biblepathwayadventures.com

INSTANT DOWNLOAD!

Moses and the Ten Plagues
Balaam's Donkey (Beginners)
Birth of the King (Beginners)
The Story of Joseph (Beginners)
Twelve Tribes of Israel (Beginners)
The Exodus (Beginners)
Noah's Ark (Beginners)
The Story of Esther (Beginners)

Made in the USA
Las Vegas, NV
31 March 2024